5/12

# THE BUSINESS
# HEALTH CHECK

Olivier Kennedy and Martin Künzi

enigma

**PROFILE
EDITIONS**

# Table
# of Contents

# About the authors

The story of Olivier and Martin started as the successful relationship between a client and his agency. Working together, these two marketing strategists soon found out that they shared a common passion: being able to go beyond branding and advertising to solve real business issues.

Olivier convinced Martin to join Enigma as a partner. Together, they grew the team, adding service designers, design strategists, and business model experts to their skilled company.

Eventually, they transformed Enigma into an all-round business consultancy with a clear mission: to help organizations be great at what they do. Or become even greater.

# Foreword

It's been 19 years since we entered the 21st century. A lot has changed: digital ubiquity, flat hierarchies, global word-of-mouth, telecommuting... You know that. We know that. But when we look around, we are baffled to see how many companies are still operating in an old-fashioned way. Most businesses don't know how to handle the deep social and behavioral changes at work right now.

For the last 10 years, we've been working with hundreds of companies. In a lot of places, we've seen problems and disorders with common patterns. We've started to call them business diseases. And we've decided to investigate.

This book is based on field study and our extensive experience with clients. It will help you diagnose the situations you might run into every day—be it in your company or among friends and acquaintances.

Keep curing!

*Olivier and Martin*

# How to make the most out of this book

This book was designed to help you keep your company healthy in the 21st century. Please use it as you would use a dictionary. Do not read it from the first page in a linear way, as it may be boring. Instead, follow any topic relevant to your industry or work context. From there, you will be able to explore related topics.

## Search with the indexes

Would you like to know what diseases you might be exposed to? Or find out which ones you already have without knowing? The best way is to navigate using the various indexes. There's an "Index by risk groups" and an "Index by frequency". Of course, if you're looking for a specific disease, you can also go for a quick search in the alphabetical indexes. Do check the end of the book for all indexes.

## Use the related diseases

Most business diseases are related to others. You should use these links to explore unexpected relations and shed light on the hidden patterns in your company or in your own behavior.

diseases of the

# nervous system

— CHAPTER 1

The nervous system allows your body to transform thoughts into actions. The nerves carry orders from the brain to various body parts. This communication, however, does not move in just one direction. Through the nervous system, the brain gets information from the body parts in return. This helps the brain understand the context and the impact of the orders it gives.

If we had a one-way nervous system, we would end up seeing people in the street walk into walls, similar to characters in old video games. This is because the body parts would have no way to tell the brain that its orders don't make any sense, and they would keep banging into the wall.

Strategy is the nervous system of any business. Strategy is about turning the vision of a company's brain into concrete action. But strategy also needs the feedback of the body parts, so that it can adjust and understand the context where this action takes place.

# Youngitis

—

"Creating only for millennials
and the younger generation, while the elderly
actually outnumber them"

**Supporting Data** | *The median age in Germany in 2016 was 46.8.*
– *Source: Statista*

| | |
|---|---|
| **Diagnosis questions** | How old are your customers? |
| | How relevant is age when it comes to your service or product? |
| | Can you base your offer on socio-graphics instead of demographics? |
| **Related diseases** | Youngitis is a specific form of Persona blindness (14) |
| **Cure** | Strategic Foresight |
| **Risk of contagion** | ● ○ ○ Low |
| **Frequency** | ● ● ○ ○ Common |
| **Underlying cause** | Managing by clichés |
| **Risk groups** | C-Level executives |
| | Marketing teams |
| | R&D departments |

# Persona blindness

—

"Not knowing who
your customers really are"

## Supporting Data

*– Source: Janrain & Harris
Interactive*

*As much as 74% of online consumers get frustrated with
websites when content (e.g. offers, ads, promotions)
appears that has nothing to do with their interests.*

| | |
|---|---|
| **Diagnosis questions** | What do you need to know about your customers? |
| | What's the best way to learn about your customers? |
| | Why not get out and actually meet them? |
| **Related diseases** | Youngitis is a specific form of Persona blindness (12) |
| **Cure** | User research |
| **Risk of contagion** | ●● ○     Medium |
| **Frequency** | ●●● ○     Widespread |
| **Underlying cause** | We know better |
| **Risk groups** | C-Level executives |
| | Marketing teams |

# Idea
# love dısorder

—

"Thinking that a great idea
is enough to build a successful offer"

## Supporting Data
– *Source: Fractl*

*The main reason that startups fail (51%) is a non-viable business model.*

| | |
|---|---|
| **Diagnosis questions** | How can you make money with your idea? |
| | Can you fight your own ideas? |
| | How come no one ever had the same idea before? |
| **Related diseases** | Stormingshitism (170) |
| | Innovation optimism (174) |
| **Cure** | Business Model Canvas |
| **Risk of contagion** | ● ● ●     High |
| **Frequency** | ● ● ○ ○     Common |
| **Underlying cause** | Managing by clichés |
| **Risk groups** | Entrepreneurs & investors |

Most businesses
don't know how to
handle the deep
social and behavioral
changes at
work right now

# Egostratitis

—

"Believing that top executives
and managers are the only ones
able to understand
and handle strategic issues"

## Supporting Data

– Source: Bridges Business
Consultancy

*As much as 60% of leaders think that less than 20% of the
workforce has at least a basic understanding of the company strategy and can explain it.*

| Diagnosis questions | Can you explain the strategy clearly enough? |
| --- | --- |
| | What does your team actually know about your strategy? |
| | Are you working with a bunch of idiots? |
| Related diseases | Cryptostrategy syndrome *(can be either a cause or a complication)* (22) |
| Cure | Team Alignment Map *(on a high dose)* |
| Risk of contagion | ●●● High (inside risk groups) |
| | ●○○ Low (outside) |
| Frequency | ●●○○ Common |
| Underlying cause | We know better |
| Risk groups | C-Level executives |
| | Managers |

# Cryptostrategy syndrome

—

"Not sharing the company strategy
with the workforce"

**Supporting Data**
– Source: Six Disciplines

*Only 27% of a typical company's employees have access
to its strategic plan.*

| Diagnosis questions | Did you run through your strategy with your team? |
| --- | --- |
| | Did you ask questions? |
| | How clear were your explanations? |
| Related diseases | Egostratitis *(can be a cause or a complication)* (20) |
| | Passive rebel syndrome (50) |
| Cure | Team Alignment Map |
| Risk of contagion | ● ○ ○          Low |
| Frequency | ● ● ● ○          Widespread |
| Underlying cause | Sadism |
| Risk groups | C-Level executives |
| | Managers |

# Strategic delirium

—

"Believing you know
the strategy well, when in fact you
can't name the priorities"

---

**Supporting Data**

– *Source: Donald Sull*

*Two-thirds of senior managers can't name their firm's top priorities.*

| Diagnosis questions | Is your strategy simple enough? |
|---|---|
| | Do you have more than three priorities? |
| | How often do you talk about your strategy with others? |
| **Related diseases** | Egostratitis (20) |
| **Cure** | Team Alignment Map |
| **Risk of contagion** | ●●● High |
| **Frequency** | ●●○○ Common |
| **Underlying cause** | We know better |
| **Risk groups** | Everyone |

# Anthropo-strategitis

—

"To let a strategy live by itself as if it were a self-conscious organism, able to develop without external input"

## Supporting Data

– *Source: Harvard Business School*

*As much as 85% of leadership teams spend less than 1 hour per month discussing strategy, while 50% spend no time at all.*

| | |
|---|---|
| **Diagnosis questions** | Did you set up a real strategy execution plan? |
| | What are the metrics to monitor the strategy execution? |
| | How actionable is your strategy? |
| **Related diseases** | Egostratitis (20) |
| **Cure** | Strategy Map |
| | Team Alignment Map |
| **Risk of contagion** | ● ● ●    High |
| **Frequency** | ● ● ● ○    Widespread |
| **Underlying cause** | Incompetence |
| **Risk groups** | C-Level executives |

Are you working with a bunch of idiots

# Strategic disbelief

—

"Believing a strategy
will most probably fail"

**Supporting Data**
– Source: Bridges Business
Consultancy

*As much as 2% of leaders are confident that they will
achieve 80–100% of their strategy's objectives.*

| Diagnosis questions | Why did you even accept this strategy? |
| --- | --- |
| | How much trust do you have in your teams? |
| | What do you think will make your strategy fail? |
| Related diseases | Passive rebel syndrome (50) |
| Cure | Team Alignment Map |
| Risk of contagion | ● ● ●    High |
| Frequency | ● ● ● ●    Out of control |
| Underlying cause | Pessimism |
| Risk groups | Managers |
| | Workforce |

# Uncausalitis

—

"Having internal teams drift
away from the company strategy"

**Supporting Data**

*– Source: Harvard Business
School*

*As much as 67% of HR and IT teams develop strategic
plans that are not linked to the organization's strategy.*

| Diagnosis questions | Do you oversee your team's objectives and action plans? |
| --- | --- |
| | What's your plan to achieve strategic alignment? |
| | How can you make sure your strategic priorities are the single compass for anything happening in the company? |
| **Related diseases** | Stormingshitism    (170) |
| **Cure** | Team Alignment Map |
| **Risk of contagion** | ● ● ●    High |
| **Frequency** | ● ● ○ ○    Common |
| **Underlying cause** | Incompetence |
| **Risk groups** | HR departments |
| | IT departments |

# Statusquoism

—

"Designing an unrealistic
strategy that will fail and eventually
preserve the status quo"

**Supporting Data**

– *Source: The Economist*

*As much as 65% of companies are "somewhat ineffective" or worse at introducing change caused by strategic initiatives.*

| | |
|---|---|
| **Diagnosis questions** | Do you really want the changes implied by your strategy? |
| | How hard do you believe in your own strategy? |
| | Why do you think your company needs to change? |
| **Related diseases** | Strategic disbelief (30) |
| **Cure** | Strategic foresight |
| **Risk of contagion** | ● ○ ○     Low |
| **Frequency** | ● ● ○ ○     Common |
| **Underlying cause** | Fear of change |
| **Risk groups** | C-Level executives |

diseases of the

# cardiovascular system

— CHAPTER 2

The cardiovascular system makes blood circulate throughout the body. This circulation is essential to transport, for instance, nutrients or oxygen to the body cells. The cardiovascular system also helps the body fight diseases and stabilize its own temperature.

When blood pressure is too high, it usually has no visible symptoms at first. But over time, if untreated, it can cause unpleasant conditions, such as heart disease and strokes. Before modern medicine, it was widely accepted that drawing blood out of a sick body would help. Now, we know better.

The workforce is the cardiovascular system of an organization. Similar to the circulation of blood, it helps send information through departments. An effective workforce will also drive the fight against competitors.

A healthy workforce makes it possible for a business to find a new balance in an ever-changing world. On the other hand, bloodletting works here just as inefficiently as with actual bodies.

Only 2% of leaders
are confident
that they will achieve
80–100% of
their strategy's objectives

# Salaryısm

—

"Believing that money
is the primary performance
driver for your teams"

## Supporting Data
– *Source: Socialcast*

*As much as 69% of employees would work harder if they
felt their efforts were better appreciated.*

| Diagnosis questions | Do you know what any of your team members thinks about their salaries? |
|---|---|
| | What can you do so that your people feel like their work is appreciated? |
| | How often do you speak to your employees about their work? |
| Related diseases | Monetary solutionism ⓵²⁶ |
| Cure | Value Proposition Canvas |
| Risk of contagion | ● ○ ○    Low |
| Frequency | ● ● ○ ○    Common |
| Underlying cause | Managing by clichés |
| Risk groups | Managers |
| | HR departments |

# Disenchantment syndrome

—

"Not expecting anything
good or useful from
the management anymore"

## Supporting Data

– Source: Quantum
Workplace

As much as 21% of employees are not confident that their manager will provide regular, constructive feedback.

| | |
|---|---|
| **Diagnosis questions** | Do you know how your team feels about your management? |
| | How actionable and socially acceptable is your feedback? |
| | Do you treat all employees equally? |
| **Related diseases** | Strategic disbelief (30) |
| **Cure** | Talk with your team |
| | Team Alignment Map |
| **Risk of contagion** | ● ● ●  High |
| **Frequency** | ● ○ ○ ○  Rare |
| **Underlying cause** | Pessimism |
| **Risk groups** | Workforce |

# Managerial assessitis

—

"Believing that only a manager
can effectively assess
the work of an employee"

## Supporting Data
*– Source: Globoforce*

*As much as 41% of companies that use peer-to-peer recognition have seen positive increases in customer satisfaction.*

| Diagnosis questions | Who is to review your employees' performance? |
|---|---|
| | Do you really know what all your team members are doing? |
| | How much do you trust your team? |
| **Related diseases** | Egostratitis (20) |
| **Cure** | Peer-to-peer assessments |
| **Risk of contagion** | ●●● High |
| **Frequency** | ●● ○○ Common |
| **Underlying cause** | We know better |
| **Risk groups** | HR departments |
| | Managers |

# Procrastignition

—

"Believing that feedback
needs a formal, periodic setting
to be effective"

**Supporting Data**
– *Source: PwC*

*As much as 80% of Gen Y say that they prefer on-the-spot recognition over formal reviews.*

| | |
|---|---|
| **Diagnosis questions** | How often are you giving feedback to your employees? |
| | What's the best moment to recognize when someone has done great work? |
| | How can you make sure that you won't forget to say something if you wait till the next formal occasion? |
| **Related diseases** | Egostratitis (20) |
| | Managerial assessitis (44) |
| **Cure** | On-the-spot recognition |
| | Micro-reviews |
| **Risk of contagion** | ●●● High |
| **Frequency** | ●●○○ Common |
| **Underlying cause** | Managing by clichés |
| **Risk groups** | HR departments |
| | Managers |

A healthy workforce
makes it possible
for a business to find
a new balance in
an ever-changing world

# Passive rebel syndrome

—

"Not believing in your process
but using it anyway"

## Supporting Data

*– Source: Deloitte*

*Only 8% of companies believe that their performance management process is highly effective in driving business value, while 58% say that it's not an effective use of time.*

| | |
|---|---|
| **Diagnosis questions** | Would you use a broken appliance at home? |
| | Who are you afraid to provoke? |
| | Who can you share your doubts with? |
| **Related diseases** | Cryptostrategy syndrome  (22) |
| | Strategic disbelief  (30) |
| **Cure** | Talk to your staff |
| **Risk of contagion** | ●●● High |
| **Frequency** | ●●○○ Common |
| **Underlying cause** | Pessimism |
| **Risk groups** | Workforce |

# Robotic phantasm

—

"Treating your employees
as machines without
human needs and behaviors"

## Supporting Data
– *Source: Atlassian*

*The average employee experiences 56 interruptions a day; that's 1 every eight-and-a-half minutes.*

| Diagnosis questions | How would you react if you were in the other person's shoes? |
|---|---|
| | What can you do to be more human toward others? |
| | How often do you take some time to build a relationship with team members? |
| **Related diseases** | Egostratitis (20) |
| **Cure** | Be the employee for a day |
| **Risk of contagion** | ●○○  Low |
| **Frequency** | ●●●○  Widespread |
| **Underlying cause** | Lack of empathy |
| **Risk groups** | C-Level executives |
| | Managers |

# Multitasking mania

—

"Believing that multitasking is an efficient working model"

**Supporting Data**
– Source: Atlassian

On average, an employee spends only 3 minutes on one task before moving to another.

| | |
|---|---|
| **Diagnosis questions** | Have you ever tried to replace any of your team? |
| | How many times are you switching tasks? |
| | How often a day do you feel the need to focus on a single task? |
| **Related diseases** | Compulsive email disorder ⑦⓪ |
| **Cure** | Plan focus moments in calendar |
| **Risk of contagion** | ● ● ●    High |
| **Frequency** | ● ● ● ●    Out of control |
| **Underlying cause** | Managing by clichés |
| **Risk groups** | Managers |
| | Workforce |

# Coolness syndrome

—

## "Taking cool for creative-friendly"

**Supporting Data**

– *Source: Business News Daily*

*Despite the recent trend toward open-plan offices, 60% of creatives say that they are most creative in private environments.*

| Diagnosis questions | What does it mean to be creative? |
| --- | --- |
| | Do your people care about cool? |
| | Do you know the difference between creativity and innovation? |
| Related diseases | Innovation optimism (174) |
| Cure | Look at behavioral science studies to see what makes people really creative |
| Risk of contagion | ●○○ Low |
| Frequency | ●●○○ Common |
| Underlying cause | Managing by clichés |
| Risk groups | Creative industry |
| | Marketing teams |

# 80%

of Gen Y say
that they prefer on-the-spot
recognition
over formal reviews

2.9.

# 9 to 5 syndrome

—

"The workweek being simply
a survival challenge
between two weekends"

**Supporting Data**
– *Source: Salary.com*

*As much as 73% of American workers work solely for the paycheck.*

| | |
|---|---|
| **Diagnosis questions** | What makes your people get out of bed in the morning? |
| | Can you identify who in your teams is disengaged? |
| | How can you help them re-engage? |
| **Related diseases** | Disenchantment syndrome (42) |
| **Cure** | Cultural footprint |
| **Risk of contagion** | ●●○　　Medium |
| **Frequency** | ●●●○　Widespread |
| **Underlying cause** | Pessimism |
| **Risk groups** | Everyone |

# Turnover delirium

—

"Believing that replacing employees
is quick and easy"

## Supporting Data

– Source: UNC Kenan–
Flagler Business School

Turnover, which often follows a long-term disengage-
ment, costs organizations between 48% and 61% of an
employee's annual salary.

| | |
|---|---|
| **Diagnosis questions** | Are you sure there are people out there ready to work for you? |
| | How valuable is an employee's know-how and company experience? |
| | How easily can you have people switch positions inside the company? |
| **Related diseases** | Automation negativism (154) |
| | Customerbot infection (144) |
| | Robotic phantasm (52) |
| **Cure** | Review your internal data about turnover effects |
| **Risk of contagion** | ● ○ ○  Low |
| **Frequency** | ● ● ○ ○  Common |
| **Underlying cause** | We know better |
| **Risk groups** | C-Level Executives |
| | Managers |

# Schooling syndrome

—

"Not being able to keep
the younger generation in your company
once they have learned
what they wanted to learn"

## Supporting Data

– Source: US Bureau of
Labor Statistics

*The median tenure of workers age 55 to 64 is 10.4 years.
When it came to workers age 25 to 34, that number drops
drastically to 3 years.*

| | |
|---|---|
| **Diagnosis questions** | Do you know what your employees expect from their time in your company? |
| | What are you doing to keep talents inside? |
| | How long are people staying in your company compared to your competitors? |
| **Related diseases** | Youngitis (12) |
| | Turnover delirium (62) |
| **Cure** | Cultural footprint |
| **Risk of contagion** | ● ● ○    Medium |
| **Frequency** | ● ● ● ○    Widespread |
| **Underlying cause** | Lack of empathy |
| **Risk groups** | Highly demanding jobs |
| | Young workforce |

# Meeting virus

—

"Overusing meetings in a company
– a disease that tends
to get worse with time"

## Supporting Data
*– Source: Atlassian*

As much as 37 billion dollars of salary are lost in unnecessary meetings in US businesses.

| | |
|---|---|
| **Diagnosis questions** | Is a meeting the best way to get things moving? |
| | How can you make meetings more productive? |
| | How seriously do you take any meeting? |
| **Related diseases** | 9 to 5 syndrome (60) |
| | Compulsive email disorder (70) |
| | Multitasking mania (54) |
| **Cure** | Remote work |
| | Asynchronous collaborative tools |
| **Risk of contagion** | ● ● ●   High |
| **Frequency** | ● ● ● ●   Out of control |
| **Underlying cause** | Managing by clichés |
| **Risk groups** | Everyone |

On
average,
an
employee
experiences
56
interruptions
a
day

1 2 3 4 5 6 7 8 9 10
11 12 13 14 15 16 17 18
19 20 21 22 23 24
25 26 27 28 29 30 31
32 33 34 35 36 37
38 39 40 41 42 43 44
45 46 47 48 49
50 51 52 53 54 55 **56**

# Compulsive email disorder

—

"Spending
a disproportionate part
of a workday
handling emails"

**Supporting Data**
– Source: Atlassian

*On average, an employee checks their emails 36 times an hour.*

| | |
|---|---|
| **Diagnosis questions** | How many emails are really useful? |
| | How many emails are you deleting without even opening them? |
| | How many people are you CCing? |
| **Related diseases** | In case of an outburst, might lead to Multitasking mania by the management (54) |
| | Meeting virus (66) |
| **Cure** | Company chat systems |
| | Zero inbox |
| **Risk of contagion** | ● ● ●     High |
| **Frequency** | ● ● ● ●     Out of control |
| **Underlying cause** | Managing by clichés |
| **Risk groups** | Everyone |

# Daysleeping disorder

—

"Being too tired to do your work"

**Supporting Data**
– Source: Career Addict

As much as 47% of American workers have fallen asleep at work at some point during their careers.

| | |
|---|---|
| **Diagnosis questions** | How much sleep did you get last night? |
| | How often do you see people yawning? |
| | How late at night are your team members working? |
| **Related diseases** | Disenchantment syndrome (42) |
| **Cure** | Resource management |
| **Risk of contagion** | ● ○ ○      Low |
| **Frequency** | ● ● ○ ○      Common |
| **Underlying cause** | Lack of empathy |
| **Risk groups** | Highly demanding jobs |

diseases of the
# skeletal
# system

— CHAPTER 3

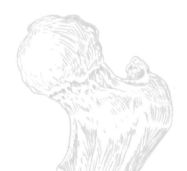

The skeletal system is the backbone that allows the body to stand. This system is often forgotten because it is hidden deep under the skin. However, this system is highly important, as it gives shape to a body that would otherwise simply be a chubby mass of grease and muscles.

In the 21st century, the digital is the skeletal system of any organization. Digital transformation is a concept of the past century. Today, digital is so widespread that we have stopped noticing it. When digital is everywhere, a business without a digital backbone is essentially a flabby shape that is unable to move forward. Basically, like jelly.

# Mobile-first obsession

—

"Blindly believing that mobile phones are always more important than desktop computers"

---

**Supporting Data**

*– Source: Adobe Digital Insights*

*A desktop visit to a retail site is worth about four times as much as a smartphone visit.*

| Diagnosis questions | When is the desktop experience better? |
| --- | --- |
| | Is the desktop experience really better or does your mobile experience really suck? |
| | What can you do to bring both desktop and mobile experience to the same level? |
| **Related diseases** | Banner optimism (110) |
| **Cure** | Google Analytics and conversion tracking |
| **Risk of contagion** | ●●○   Medium |
| **Frequency** | ●●○○   Common |
| **Underlying cause** | Technological determinism |
| **Risk groups** | Marketing teams |
| | IT departments |

# 73%

of American
workers work solely
for the paycheck

# Reading
# negationism

—

"Believing that nobody
reads anymore in the age
of video and photos"

**Supporting Data**
– Source: Hubspot

*The average consumer processes 100,500 digital words
daily.*

| | |
|---|---|
| **Diagnosis questions** | How can you stay relevant in that flow of information? |
| | What information can be shared using another medium than text? |
| | Did you just read the stat overleaf thinking "this can't be true" before realizing that you were indeed reading a lot of text? |
| **Related diseases** | When taken too much medication, might revert to Textual optimism (92) |
| **Cure** | Google Analytics |
| **Risk of contagion** | ● ● ●    High |
| **Frequency** | ● ● ○ ○    Common |
| **Underlying cause** | We know better |
| **Risk groups** | 40+ y.o. decision makers |
| | Marketing teams |

# Word of mouth positivism

—

"Believing that positive word
of mouth will be stronger
than negative word of mouth
(hint: it's the opposite)"

## Supporting Data
*– Source: American Express*

*Americans tell an average of 9 people about good experiences, and they tell 16 (nearly two times more) people about poor experiences.*

| Diagnosis questions | How can you motivate more users to spread positive word of mouth? |
|---|---|
| | How can you track negative word of mouth? |
| | How long does it take you to react to negative word of mouth? |
| Related diseases | Innovation optimism (174) |
| | Banner optimism (110) |
| | Digital optimism syndrome (160) |
| Cure | Online mention tracking |
| Risk of contagion | ● ○ ○     Low |
| Frequency | ● ● ○ ○     Common |
| Underlying cause | Blind optimism |
| Risk groups | Marketing teams |

# Criticaphobia

—

"Not allowing consumers to review
your products or services
because you fear criticism will make
you look less performant"

---

**Supporting Data**
– Source: PeopleClaim

*On-site consumer reviews can increase conversions by 74%.*

| Diagnosis questions | Where could you allow customers to provide reviews? |
|---|---|
| | Are there any external review tools that you could use that are relevant in your industry? |
| | What is your strategy to answer customer complaints in reviews? |
| **Related diseases** | Banner optimism (110) |
| **Cure** | A/B testing |
| **Risk of contagion** | ● ○ ○     Low |
| **Frequency** | ● ○ ○ ○     Rare |
| **Underlying cause** | Pessimism |
| **Risk groups** | Marketing teams |

# Opinion-building idealism

—

"Believing that consumers
and users will take
the time to explore your page before
making an opinion"

**Supporting Data**
– Source: Google

*In less than 50 milliseconds, users form an initial "gut feeling" that helps them decide whether they'll stay or leave.*

| | |
|---|---|
| **Diagnosis questions** | What will the user remember if they look at any of your marketing components for only 5 seconds? |
| | What is the key message a user should get in the first 50 milliseconds? |
| | How can you format this message so that the audience gets it in the blink of an eye? |
| **Related diseases** | Word of mouth positivism    (82) |
| **Cure** | Google Analytics |
| **Risk of contagion** | ●● ○     Medium |
| **Frequency** | ●●● ○     Widespread |
| **Underlying cause** | Blind optimism |
| **Risk groups** | C-Level executives |
| | Managers |
| | Marketing teams |

The average consumer
processes
100,500 digital words
daily

# Slow life syndrome

—

"Believing that 1 additional second or minute in a customer interaction will have no impact on the customer engagement"

**Supporting Data**
– Source: QuBit

*Slow-loading websites cost UK retailers £1.73bn in lost sales each year.*

| | |
|---|---|
| **Diagnosis questions** | How long does it take to answer a customer's email or text? |
| | How fast is your website compared to the industry leaders? |
| | What smart answers can you automate to save time with the first response? |
| **Related diseases** | Mobile-first obsession (76) |
| **Cure** | Google Analytics |
| **Risk of contagion** | ● ○ ○ Low |
| **Frequency** | ● ● ○ ○ Common |
| **Underlying cause** | Blind optimism |
| **Risk groups** | IT departments |
| | Marketing teams |

# Textual optimism

—

"Believing that textual information
is good to help people remember
key information or create interaction"

## Supporting Data
– Source: John Medina

*When people hear information, they're likely to remember only 10% of that information three days later. However, if a relevant image is paired with that same information, this goes up to 65%.*

| | |
|---|---|
| **Diagnosis questions** | What information are you sharing through text only? |
| | What long-form texts could be transformed into short videos? |
| | What can you do to help people better remember information? |
| **Related diseases** | Might be a reaction to overcured Reading negationism (80) |
| **Cure** | Visual storytelling |
| | Rich media |
| **Risk of contagion** | ●○○ Low |
| **Frequency** | ●●○○ Common |
| **Underlying cause** | Managing by clichés |
| **Risk groups** | Marketing teams |
| | Copywriters |
| | SEO experts |

# Social media denial syndrome

—

"Believing that new
social media platforms are
not used that much"

**Supporting Data**

*– Source: NewsCred
Insights*

*Snapchat users share 9,000 photos per second.*

| | |
|---|---|
| **Diagnosis questions** | Which social media platforms do you believe are ineffective? |
| | Which social media platforms do your clients use? |
| | How can you stand out in a stream of 9,000 photos per second? |
| **Related diseases** | Persona blindness (14) |
| **Cure** | Check usage and penetration statistics |
| **Risk of contagion** | ● ○ ○     Low |
| **Frequency** | ● ● ● ○     Widespread |
| **Underlying cause** | Pessimism |
| **Risk groups** | B2B companies |
| | C-Level executives |
| | Managers |

# Egoptimism

—

"Believing people
are interested in what
a brand has to say"

## Supporting Data

– Source: Content
Marketing Institute

Last year, the volume of brand-published content was up
to 35%, but consumer engagement with that content was
down by 17%. Marketers' response to this news? 77% of
the surveyed brands intend to create even more content
this year than the last.

| Diagnosis questions | What type of content would really interest your consumers? |
| --- | --- |
| | How much of your content is speaking only about you? |
| | What part of your content is actually interesting? Honestly? |
| **Related diseases** | Folloptimism (100) |
| **Cure** | User research |
| **Risk of contagion** | ●●● High |
| **Frequency** | ●●●○ Widespread |
| **Underlying cause** | Lack of empathy |
| **Risk groups** | C-Level executives |
| | Marketing teams |

Slow-loading
websites
cost UK retailers
£1.73bn
in lost sales
each year

3.10.

# Folloptimism

—

"Believing that people
will follow brands easily"

**Supporting Data**

*– Source: Buzzstream*

*As much as 50% of people follow 1 to 4 brands on social
media; 26% follow 5 to 9 brands.*

| Diagnosis questions | What incentive or gain will users get when they follow you? |
|---|---|
| | Do you really need all these social media profiles? |
| | What percentage of your customers is following you on social media? |
| Related diseases | Egoptimism �96 |
| Cure | Super Hero Branding |
| Risk of contagion | ●●● High |
| Frequency | ●●●○ Widespread |
| Underlying cause | Blind optimism |
| Risk groups | Marketing teams |

diseases of the
# endocrine system

— CHAPTER 4

The endocrine system sends messages through the body using chemical messengers. Among those are hormones, which are secreted to carry information to organs. Pheromones, another kind of messenger, are released directly into the air and affect the bodies of other individuals.

Marketing and communication departments are the endocrine system of an organization. They allow a business to share its ideas internally and spread messages outside the organization.

Pheromones are part of the seduction game between humans. Likewise, marketing is part of the seduction game between an organization and potential users or customers. Marketers beware: an excessive usage of pheromone can generate disgust, as the smell might be too strong for the person we want to seduce.

# More is more syndrome

—

"Believing that more choices
for the customer
leads to better success and
customer satisfaction"

## Supporting Data
– Source: Crazyegg

*In a comparative test, the email with the single CTA had a 42% higher clickthrough rate than the email with multiple CTAs, proving that less is more.*

| Diagnosis questions | How many choices do you offer for a specific product? |
| --- | --- |
| | On your home page, how many options does a user have to choose from? |
| | Are there areas where offering less choice would mean less work for you as a company? |
| Related diseases | Textual optimism (92) |
| Cure | A/B testing |
| Risk of contagion | ●● ○   Medium |
| Frequency | ●●●●   Out of control |
| Underlying cause | Managing by clichés |
| Risk groups | C-Level executives with decision-making issues |

# Compulsive social media disorder

—

"Blindly believing
that social media is the only efficient
digital marketing channel"

**Supporting Data**

– Source: Emailexpert

*For every $1 spent on email marketing, the average return is $44.25.*

| | |
|---|---|
| **Diagnosis questions** | What are the unattractive but highly effective marketing actions in your industry? |
| | Do you know the ROI of every marketing action you have implemented in the last three years? |
| | What is the cost of social media today in your company? |
| **Related diseases** | Folloptimism (100) |
| | Mobile-first obsession (76) |
| | Banner optimism (110) |
| **Cure** | A/B testing |
| **Risk of contagion** | ●● ○   Medium |
| **Frequency** | ●● ○ ○   Common |
| **Underlying cause** | Managing by clichés |
| **Risk groups** | Community managers |
| | Marketing teams |

Snapchat users
share 9,000 photos
per second

# Banner optimism

—

"Believing advertising can create trust about your products and services"

| | |
|---|---|
| **Diagnosis questions** | What is your goal with advertising? |
| | What will help you attain more trust from your customers? |
| | Which marketing technique is best for your specific industry? |
| **Related diseases** | Compulsive social media disorder (106) |
| | Word of mouth positivism (82) |
| | Mobile-first obsession (76) |
| | Criticaphobia (84) |
| **Cure** | User research |
| **Risk of contagion** | ● ● ○  Medium |
| **Frequency** | ● ○ ○ ○  Rare |
| **Underlying cause** | Lack of empathy |
| **Risk groups** | C-Level executives |
| | Marketing teams |

# Impact disillusionism

—

"Believing that a system can produce higher results with the same old methodology"

**Supporting Data**
– Source: Episerver

*96% of non-agile marketers want to do more with the same team.*

| Diagnosis questions | What are the big changes you are working on? |
|---|---|
| | What new methodologies and working models are you going to implement? |
| | Are there processes where you continue to get the same negative results but keep them anyway? |
| Related diseases | Imperfection blindness (136) |
| | Trainee infection (130) |
| Cure | Being serious? |
| Risk of contagion | ● ● ●    High |
| Frequency | ● ● ● ●    Out of control |
| Underlying cause | Incompetence |
| Risk groups | Managers |

# Voidfilling mania

—

"Using filling words or clichés
to hide the fact that you have,
in reality, nothing to say"

**Supporting Data**
– *Source: NeuroImage*

*Action words or sensory words engage with larger parts
of the brain than overused phrases such as "a rough day"
or "one in a million."*

| | |
|---|---|
| **Diagnosis questions** | Who is in charge of reviewing the number of clichés in your company communication? |
| | Which sentences or overused phrases in your industry should you avoid? |
| | Did you test the impact of clichés on engagement with your content? |
| **Related diseases** | Textual optimism (92) |
| | Big is beautiful syndrome (124) |
| **Cure** | Use a second reader as a bullshit detector |
| **Risk of contagion** | ●●● High |
| **Frequency** | ●●●○ Widespread |
| **Underlying cause** | Incompetence |
| **Risk groups** | Marketing teams |
| | Sales departments |
| | Amateur copywriters |

diseases of the

# decision-making system

— CHAPTER 5

According to behavioral psychologist Daniel Kahneman, the decision-making system is composed of two sub-systems: "System 1" and "System 2". Yes, Nobel Prize winners may be smart, but they suck at naming things. System 1 is the fast and automatic brain system. It follows an intuitive approach. System 2, on the other hand, is a slower, analytical brain system where reason dominates.

In an organization, customer experience is the decision-making system. For a long time, businesses have relied mainly on System 1, leveraging intuition and flair to achieve success. However, 21st-century organizations have learned to master System 2, using the customer voice to inform a data-driven, more analytical decision-making process.

Marketing is part
of the seduction game
between
an organization
and potential
users or customers

# Personalization disbelief

—

"Believing that people
don't care that
we remember their name"

**Supporting Data**
– Source: Experian

Personalized emails deliver six times higher transaction
rates, but 70% of brands fail to use them.

| | |
|---|---|
| **Diagnosis questions** | In what database did you hide the customers' names? |
| | What is the cost of bringing these data into action for personalization? |
| | When should your staff ask for names in the customer journey? |
| **Related diseases** | Customerbot infection (144) |
| **Cure** | Better CRMs |
| **Risk of contagion** | ● ○ ○     Low |
| **Frequency** | ● ● ○ ○     Common |
| **Underlying cause** | Lack of empathy |
| **Risk groups** | Marketing teams |
| | Support departments |

# Data and tools solutionism

—

"Believing you need plenty of
data and tools to create
a great customer experience"

---

## Supporting Data

– Source: Forrester
Research

As much as 77% of people say that valuing their time is the
most important thing a company can do to provide them
with good service.

| | |
|---|---|
| **Diagnosis questions** | What tools and processes are you waiting for? |
| | What can you do today to improve the customer experience, without new processes and tools? |
| | How can you show your customers that you value their time? |
| **Related diseases** | Robotic phantasm (52) |
| **Cure** | Talk to your customers |
| **Risk of contagion** | ●●● High |
| **Frequency** | ●●●○ Widespread |
| **Underlying cause** | Technological determinism |
| **Risk groups** | Geeky managers |
| | IT departments |

# Big is beautiful syndrome

—

"Believing that appearing
as a huge group will create more
trust in the customer's mind"

**Supporting Data**
– *Source: American Express*

*As much as 80% of Americans agree that smaller comp-
anies place a greater emphasis on customer service than
large businesses.*

| | |
|---|---|
| **Diagnosis questions** | What are your usual ways to build trust? |
| | Do these trust-building techniques actually work? |
| | How can you value your smaller size to your customers? |
| **Related diseases** | Voidfilling mania (114) |
| **Cure** | Humility |
| **Risk of contagion** | ●●○ Medium |
| **Frequency** | ●●○○ Common |
| **Underlying cause** | We know better |
| **Risk groups** | C-Level executives |
| | Sales departments |
| | SMBs |

# Monetary solutionism

—

"Forgetting that relations
are built through emotions,
not monetary incentives"

## Supporting Data
– Source: Liveperson

As much as 37% of customers are satisfied with service
recovery when they are offered something of monetary
value (e.g. a refund or credit). However, when the business adds an apology on top of the compensation, the
customer satisfaction doubles to 74%.

| Diagnosis questions | Where can you add emotion in your relationship with your customers? |
| --- | --- |
| | What might function as a token of emotion? |
| | When was the last time you apologized to a customer? |
| Related diseases | Salaryism              .    (40) |
| Cure | Value Proposition Canvas |
| Risk of contagion | ●●●      High |
| Frequency | ●●○○      Common |
| Underlying cause | Lack of empathy |
| Risk groups | Marketing teams |

# 80%

of Americans agree
that smaller
companies place a greater
emphasis on
customer service than
large businesses

# Trainee infection

—

"Believing that customer service
staff members don't need
to be specialists on the topic"

**Supporting Data**

– Source: Helpscout

When asked about why they'd given up on a company's
customer support, 73% of customers cited incompetent
(and rude) replies as their primary reason.

| | |
|---|---|
| **Diagnosis questions** | How big is the part of non-specialists in your support staff? |
| | How long does it take a customer to get to a specialist in your company? |
| | How many people does a customer have to go through before they reach a specialist? |
| **Related diseases** | Imperfection blindness (136) |
| **Cure** | Mystery shopper |
| **Risk of contagion** | ●●● High |
| **Frequency** | ●●○○ Common |
| **Underlying cause** | We know better |
| **Risk groups** | C-Level executives |
| | Support departments |

# Back together blindness

—

"Believing it's easy
to fix a broken relationship
with a customer"

### Supporting Data

– Source: "Understanding
Customers" by
Ruby Newell-Legner

*It takes 12 positive experiences to make up for one un-
resolved negative experience.*

| | |
|---|---|
| **Diagnosis questions** | How many positive experiences do you create after you messed up with a client? |
| | What are the typical unresolved negative experiences in your service? |
| | What inexpensive and human positive experiences can you create to overcome a bad one? |
| **Related diseases** | Imperfection blindness (136) |
| | Word of mouth positivism (82) |
| **Cure** | Talk to your customers |
| **Risk of contagion** | ●●●  High |
| **Frequency** | ●●○○  Common |
| **Underlying cause** | Lack of empathy |
| **Risk groups** | Support departments |

# Service deafness

—

"Not listening to customer feedback and not even searching for this type of feedback"

A typical business hears from 4% of its dissatisfied customers.

| Diagnosis questions | Where do your users share their complaints without you asking for it? |
| --- | --- |
| | How can you better manage customer feedback? |
| | Who in your company should be in charge of talking to the customers? |
| Related diseases | Expectation blindness (140) |
| | Trainee infection (130) |
| Cure | Net Promoter Score surveys |
| Risk of contagion | ●●● High |
| Frequency | ●●○○ Common |
| Underlying cause | We know better |
| Risk groups | Marketing teams |
| | Support departments |

# Imperfection blindness

—

"Believing you are at the top level in
any quality, while feedback
from the majority of your customers
tell the opposite"

## Supporting Data

– Source: Lee Resources

*As much as 80% of companies say that they deliver
"superior" customer service whereas only 8% of people are of the opinion that these same companies deliver
"superior" customer service.*

| Diagnosis questions | In what topics or qualities are you blind about your imperfections? |
| --- | --- |
| | What errors are most mentioned by your customers? |
| | Which wrong KPIs make you believe that you have a good customer service when in fact you don't? |
| Related diseases | Trainee infection (130) |
| Cure | User research |
| Risk of contagion | ● ● ○     Medium |
| Frequency | ● ● ● ●     Out of control |
| Underlying cause | We know better |
| Risk groups | C–Level executives |

# 73%

When asked about
why they'd given up on
a company's
customer support, 73%
of customers
cited incompetent
(and rude) replies
as their primary reason

# Expectation blindness

—

"Not knowing or meeting
the customers' expectations"

## Supporting Data

– Source: Forrester
Research

As much as 41% of consumers expect an email response
within six hours. Only 36% of retailers have responded
that quickly.

| | |
|---|---|
| **Diagnosis questions** | How can you ask your customers about their opinions in a quantitative manner? |
| | What qualitative methods will you use to find out why users are frustrated? |
| | Which users should you ask for feedback first? |
| **Related diseases** | Service deafness (134) |
| **Cure** | User research |
| **Risk of contagion** | ●●● High |
| **Frequency** | ●●○○ Common |
| **Underlying cause** | We know better |
| **Risk groups** | Everyone |

diseases of the

# respiratory
# system

— CHAPTER 6

A biologist might define the respiratory system as a group of specific organs and structures used for gas exchange. Regular people usually refer to it as breathing, which makes it slightly easier to grasp. Our body needs oxygen to perform every function, such as digesting food, moving muscles, or even just thinking.

Information technology is the respiratory system of an organization. Just as with bodies, a business constantly needs to draw new data in to be able to continue evaluating the context and, therefore, working. If you run out of air, you'll be dead in a few minutes. If you don't get new data about what's happening... well, you get the picture.

# Customerbot infection

—

"Handling your customers
as robots who don't
need human emotions in their
relationship with you"

## Supporting Data
*– Source: American Express*

*As much as 67% of customers have hung up the phone out of frustration when they could not talk to a real person.*

| | |
|---|---|
| **Diagnosis questions** | Where are you talking with clients as if they were robots? |
| | What can you do so that people understand that you are human? |
| | How can you bring your customers to a real person faster? |
| **Related diseases** | Robotic phantasm (52) |
| | Data and tools solutionism (122) |
| **Cure** | User research |
| **Risk of contagion** | ●○○ Low |
| **Frequency** | ●●○○ Common |
| **Underlying cause** | Lack of empathy |
| **Risk groups** | IT departments |

# Allhumanitis

—

"Refusing to see that some
interactions dealt with
by humans can be automated"

**Supporting Data**
– Source: Groove

*A three-person customer support team can save 600
hours per year through automation.*

| | |
|---|---|
| **Diagnosis questions** | Do you avoid automation because you fear you would be useless? |
| | What will you do with the time you save with automation? |
| | How can you use the time saved by automation to interact more humanly with your users? |
| **Related diseases** | In case of overmedication, can revert to Customerbot infection (144) |
| **Cure** | Talk to your IT |
| **Risk of contagion** | ● ○ ○     Low |
| **Frequency** | ● ● ○ ○     Common |
| **Underlying cause** | We know better |
| **Risk groups** | Support departments |

As much as
41% of consumers
expect an
email response within
six hours

Only 36%
of retailers
have responded
that quickly

# Mixed feelings infection

—

"Believing in the power of
massive amounts of data but being
afraid of its quantity"

## Supporting Data

– Source: Siliconangle

*The vast majority of managers are swimming in data, with 93% saying that they find it a challenge to integrate and manage all their data, and 40% describing it as "very challenging."*

| Diagnosis questions | Are you the right person to handle data? |
| --- | --- |
| | Why are you so afraid of data? |
| | Who can you employ to make sense of the data you already have? |
| Related diseases | Data and tools solutionism (122) |
| Cure | Hire a chief data scientist |
| Risk of contagion | ● ○ ○  Low |
| Frequency | ● ● ● ○  Widespread |
| Underlying cause | Incompetence |
| Risk groups | Marketing teams |

# Laggardism

—

"Waiting for a trend
to be so widespread
that all competent employees
are already hired
by some other company"

## Supporting Data

– Source: McKinsey &
Company

*There will be a shortage of talent necessary for organizations to take advantage of big data. By 2018, the United States alone could face a shortage of 140,000 to 190,000 people with deep analytical skills, as well as 1.5 million managers and analysts with the know-how to use the analysis of big data to make effective decisions.*

| | |
|---|---|
| **Diagnosis questions** | What trends are you planning to implement in the mid-term? |
| | What types of talents do you need to secure today for tomorrow? |
| | What key trends will be a competitive advantage in the next five years? |
| **Related diseases** | Service deafness (134) |
| **Cure** | Strategic foresight |
| **Risk of contagion** | ● ● ○     Medium |
| **Frequency** | ● ● ○ ○     Common |
| **Underlying cause** | Lack of confidence |
| **Risk groups** | C-Level executives |
| | Managers |

# Automation negativism

—

"Believing that automation
will lead to the end of
the world as we know it and
make everything bad"

**Supporting Data**
– Source: Forrester

*While 16% of US jobs will be lost over the next decade as a result of artificial intelligence and technology, 13.6 million jobs will be created during that time due to the trend.*

| Diagnosis questions | Why are you so pessimistic about technology? |
|---|---|
| | Are there other areas where your pessimism is blocking innovation? |
| | Where can you stop technology to avoid the catastrophic scenario you have in mind? |
| **Related diseases** | Data and tools solutionism (122) |
| | f-AI-kism (156) |
| **Cure** | Strategic foresight |
| **Risk of contagion** | ●● ○   Medium |
| **Frequency** | ●● ○ ○   Common |
| **Underlying cause** | Pessimism |
| **Risk groups** | IT departments |
| | Non-technical workforce |

6.6.

# f-AI-kısm

—

"Believing you are
using artificial intelligence (AI)
or machine learning (ML)
while it's just old-fashioned automation"

**Supporting Data**
– Source: Forrester

*Marketers' lack of understanding of AI-driven marketing might be influencing the rate of its adoption. To wit, more than 40% of participants said that they thought they had already adopted AI-driven marketing, reflecting a belief that their targeting capabilities and automation meant that AI was operating behind the scenes.*

| Diagnosis questions | Do you really know what AI is? |
|---|---|
| | Why are you so obsessed about "looking" innovative? |
| | What could real Artificial Intelligence do for you? |
| Related diseases | Automation negativism (154) |
| | Data and tools solutionism (122) |
| Cure | Talk to your IT |
| | Digital transformation |
| Risk of contagion | ●●● High |
| Frequency | ●●○○ Common |
| Underlying cause | Incompetence |
| Risk groups | Marketing teams |
| | Managers |

Just as with our bodies,
a business constantly
needs to draw new data in
to be able to continue
evaluating the context and,
therefore, working

# Digital optimism syndrome

—

"Believing that implementing a digital transformation will be quick and easy"

**Supporting Data**
*– Source: Progress*

As much as 55% of companies without an existing digital transformation program say that the timeframe to adopt one is a year or less.

| | |
|---|---|
| **Diagnosis questions** | Who can you hire as a coach for digital transformation? |
| | How long did companies in your industry take for their own digital transformation? |
| | How long have you been saying that you'll work on your digital transformation next year? |
| **Related diseases** | Innovation optimism (174) |
| **Cure** | Talk to your IT or CTO |
| **Risk of contagion** | ●● ○  Medium |
| **Frequency** | ●● ○ ○  Common |
| **Underlying cause** | Blind optimism |
| **Risk groups** | C-Level executives |
| | Marketing teams |

# Ownership syndrome

—

"Fighting for ownership of
an idea instead
of actually implementing
the idea or strategy"

## Supporting Data

– Source: Forrester

As much as 43% of organizations with a mature digital strategy see internal departments competing to
own digital as the most significant barrier to digital
transformation.

| | |
|---|---|
| **Diagnosis questions** | Who is fighting for ownership in your company? |
| | What other than ownership can you offer to get people back to work? |
| | How can you detect internal ownership fights within the company? |
| **Related diseases** | Cryptostrategy syndrome (22) |
| **Cure** | Team Alignment Map |
| **Risk of contagion** | ●● ○  Medium |
| **Frequency** | ●● ○ ○  Common |
| **Underlying cause** | Incompetence |
| **Risk groups** | C-Level executives |
| | Managers |

# reproductive system

— CHAPTER 7

In the human body, the reproductive system is composed of all the parts involved in the production of offspring. For the sake of selling this book without trouble, let's assume that most of you won't need any pictures.

This system is a key component of any lifeform. Without the reproductive system, species would not have undergone evolution. And, of course, they wouldn't be able to survive.

In business, the reproductive system is the activities and skills required to innovate. Any business has to evolve with time, make the most of new opportunities, and adapt to new contexts and habits. Just as there is no life without reproduction, there cannot be a sustainable business without innovation.

# Feature syndrome

—

"Believing that innovation
needs to be focused on product features
and not on the larger impact"

**Supporting Data**
– Source: Edelman

As much as 90% of customers agree that brand innovation needs to impact society.

| Diagnosis questions | What is the impact of your innovation on society? |
|---|---|
| | Do you talk about the societal impact of your innovation? |
| | How can you translate features into impact stories? |
| Related diseases | Idea love disorder (16) |
| Cure | User research |
| Risk of contagion | ●●● High |
| Frequency | ●●○○ Common |
| Underlying cause | Lack of empathy |
| Risk groups | R&D departments |
| | Marketing teams |

55% of companies without an existing digital transformation program say that the timeframe to adopt one is a year or less

# Stormingshitism

—

"Believing
that group brainstorming
is the best way
to get original ideas"

**Supporting Data**

*– Source: Basic and Applied
Social Psychology*

Individuals will generate more original ideas when they
don't interact with others.

| | |
|---|---|
| **Diagnosis questions** | Did you test multiple ways to generate ideas? |
| | How can you use individual idea generation to solve internal problems? |
| | How can you debunk other innovation myths inside your company? |
| **Related diseases** | Idea love disorder (16) |
| **Cure** | Silent brainstorming |
| **Risk of contagion** | ●●● High |
| **Frequency** | ●●●○ Widespread |
| **Underlying cause** | Managing by clichés |
| **Risk groups** | Marketing teams |
| | Managers |

7.3.

# Patriotic pessimism

—

"Believing that the country
you are living in
is worse than it actually is"

**Supporting Data**

– Source: Global Innova-
tion Index

Switzerland is the world's most innovative country for the
seventh time in a row.

| | |
|---|---|
| **Diagnosis questions** | How can you be prouder of your patriotic innovation status? |
| | Are your colleagues under a form of patriotic pessimism where they can't see how innovative their company is? |
| | What does being innovative mean to you? |
| **Related diseases** | Automation negativism (154) |
| **Cure** | Read studies |
| **Risk of contagion** | ●●● High |
| **Frequency** | ●●●○ Widespread |
| **Underlying cause** | Pessimism |
| **Risk groups** | Everyone |

# Innovation optimism

—

"Believing your innovation
will be successful
because you have a great idea"

**Supporting Data**

*– Source: Harvard Business School*

*As much as 95% of new customer products fail.*

| | |
|---|---|
| **Diagnosis questions** | What other parameters can you take into account to evaluate innovation? |
| | What is the business model for your next innovation project? |
| | Are you ready to fail with grace? |
| **Related diseases** | Idea love disorder      (16) |
| **Cure** | Business Model Canvas |
| | Strategic foresight |
| **Risk of contagion** | ●●●     High |
| **Frequency** | ●●○○     Common |
| **Underlying cause** | Managing by clichés |
| **Risk groups** | C-Level executives |
| | R&D departments |

# Index by contagion risk

# Index by frequency

## Rare

## Common

## Widespread

## Out of control

# Index by underlying cause

## Managing by clichés

## We know better

## Lack of empathy

## Pessimism

## Incompetence

## Blind optimism

## Technological determinism

## Sadism

## Fear of change

## Lack of confidence

# Index by
# risk groups

# Alphabetical index

# S

# T

# U

# V

# W

# Y

# Number

# Impressum

Publishing date

The first edition was published in April 2019

Authors

Olivier Kennedy and Martin Künzi

Project coordinator

Emilie Lassausaie

Based on research by the Enigma Lab

Romain Pittet and Daniele Catalanotto

Graphic design

Daniele Catalanotto and Jéromine Beuchat

Illustrations

Marc Philippin

**First published in Great Britain in 2019**
**by Profile Editions, an imprint of**
**PROFILE BOOKS LTD**
3 Holford Yard
Bevin Way
London WC1X 9HD
**www.profileeditions.com**

A CIP catalogue record for this book is available
from the British Library.

**ISBN 978 1 78816 376 7**